Isaksen, Hofsløk

CW00797933

THE LIGI

Silje Hostved Isaksen,
Marie Hofsløkken & Liv Christin Markussen
www.fortunalife.no

ISBN: 1466396946
ISBN-13: 978-1466396944

THANKS!

This book has come together through the escapades of life and through the people we have met on our way. A special thanks goes to Lilli Bendriss. She has, with her heart in the right place, guided us safely to a platform consisting of inner peace and calm. From this, our courage and trust in ourselves have grown strong. A big thanks shall also be directed to Camillo Løken, who has contributed with bringing our two worlds together, despite differences in the perception of truth and theories. Because of his work there has been built a bridge between science and faith, a bridge that we dare to cross.

Not forgetting our families and friends, who also deserves a big thank you for sticking by us, motivating us and helping us through our difficult and emotional growth. And last but not least, a great THANK YOU for letting us be channels for the knowledge that yet again shall bring the people together.

FOREWORD

The purpose of the book is to function as a tool for people to retrieve and relight their flame within. This flame connects you to the Source. It creates a sense of wholeness and balance on both inner and outer plain. The authors have received the content of the book through channeling over time. The channeling have come from the Source through different channels. Symbols and texts have been written down just as they were received without any adjustments. The drawings are depicted in their naivety and how they were drawn by the person who they were channeled by. The channels which gave us information are listed in the back of the book. The Council of Elders has been supervising the creation of the book.

~Words of wisdom~

To become a star
you have to shine
your own light,
follow your own path
and do not be afraid
of the darkness,
its only then
that a star
shines its brightest.

Isaksen, Hofsløkken & Markussen

CONTENTS

1 Introduction to the light   1

   Symbol of the light within   2

                                           3

2 The forgotten history of light   3

   The light of all times   3

   Symbol of light   10

3 The light worker   14

   How to be a light worker   14

   The light carrier   21

   The symbol of the light carrier   21

   How to live with the light   22

   Fight you own battle   25

   The Northern light, a meditation   26

4 How to reach the light   30

   Your own will   30

   Diet for a light worker   33

   Keep focus   35

   Light particles and crossroads   36

Forgotten wisdom will reoccur 37

Affirmation to get in touch with the light 39

5 Elements of the light

The thoughts 41

The ego 41

Symbol of the DNA changing 44

The balance 45

Rhythm 45

Breathe 46

Love 46

The weapon of love 47

Symbol of divine light of love 49

Divine love is the key 53

Light and water 54

The ice cube 54

Trees 58

Dolphins 58

Gratitude 59

Darkness and Despair 60

Meditation; create a friendship with your
pain 60

62

Liberation 64

Information 67

Change and accept 67

Language of Light 69

The Roses 70

Rose garden – a meditation 72

6 The symbols and their meaning 75

Frequency- sound 75

Symbol of sound 76

Water 78

Symbol of water 79

Meditation: The underwater tunnel 81

7 Wisdom from beyond 84

An amazing star, on the earth's rainbow

is what you are 84

Message from a higher self 87

The drums of war will fade 90

See the world through a grain of sand 93

Destination Star 15 97

Symbol of wisdom 98

Symbol of Star 15   107

Sharak, torch carrier for Star 15   108

Symbol of the holy grail   108

Meditation from the White Eagle   111

The Dolphin Spirit   113

You are the one you believe   119

The sparkle of the Dolphins   123

Wisdom from Nefertiti   130

Keywords to understanding the light   138

A good healer and a less good healer   142

The journey ahead, dear light worker   144

8 Channeled information about books to
   come and our work   147

   The Owl man, The Book of Life   147

   Meditation: The journey to the
   Fire in your heart   154

The writing process   157

The sources   160

The Light Within

1. INTRODUCTION TO THE LIGHT

The light of the North, a divine light born to relight every flame in every human, in every human who has forgotten the light. The light of the North vibrates on high frequencies and are spreading love, divine love. The light of the North is a treasure in every human heart, like it has always been.

Relight your flame in order to shine! Shine on every cell in your body. The light is an activator and will kick start lost and new found knowledge written in your DNA.

The light of the North is to reconcile and reunite. The light of the North: a light of love. The light from North, do you remember? The light of the North lies within every human heart. The light from the North is the dawning rebirth of lost knowledge. Long forgotten by most and remembered by the few. The light from the North is the sparkling rays from the children of the light, sent from the universe to awaken humanity. The light from the North is made possible through the genuine heart of love from which every human is born. Let the Northern Light shine down on the Earth people. Let the northern peace and tranquility shape and mold. Let the northern way of speaking and acting guide you. The northern people shine a light, a lantern of love.

"Symbol of the light within"

2. THE FORGOTTEN HISTORY OF LIGHT

The Light of all Times

From The Beginning there was light. Light has always been, it will always be. Every living particle needs light. Every particle exists because of the light. Even darkness is of pure light. Without light there will be no darkness.

During the Atlantic times, the Atlantic people used light to communicate, to understand each other, to keep peace and to practice divine love within their hearts and among each other. They used light in every way you cannot think of. Even for food, for healing, for surgery and for higher vibrations. Even underwater there was light. The Atlantic people lost the power of light when their ego grew so big that there was no other space left. No space for love or light. There were large rooms for surgery. Even in the stones there where light. In every crystal there was light vibrating with a special tone.

"Teacher of light ready to gather children by the water port"

To create balance between all there is, they used light. Between every cell, between every human, between every particle every atom, there is light.

The Atlantic people knew how to separate light. The light let them separate it. The light occurred like balls. This balls contained information and memories of all times. Much like today's memory-sticks for computers. The teacher carried a light ball in her hands. Her dress was dark blue with sparkles. Her hair was long and black and white. Her eyes were deep blue, and she was tiny and taller than humans. At the picture, she is standing at a meeting point in Atlantis, waiting for her students to arrive.

The wave took the Atlantic people. It carried them back to the land of spirits - The Destination Star 15. The wisdom of this destination will be barrier breaking in your work! Use it with respect and pure love - this is not a game! This is the new life!

The particles of the Atlantic people are very important for understanding the big picture. A lot of grief can be found within here, and a lot of terror. Phobias are orignated from here. Phobias of water, fearing of the fire, the phobia of reptiles.

During the atlantic time, all humans were in line with the nature. However some conflicts occurred. People took nature into their own hands. This was the wrong step! Nature was stronger than the humans realized. The power is stronger! In order to have dominion over nature, mankind extracted resources from the nature. This resources damaged the power of nature. Mankind did not realize this before it was to late. The power must be built up again. Nature and earth are fighters! A new change is coming, a new era will rise up. When light within heart as a true guide, the lessons are learned. Once again the lightbearers will stand up and front. They will shine their lights through though times, darkness and despair. Gaia is about to level up.

"BRUDESLØRET"

Jesus Christ of the sun was sent to bring light in every human heart. back then, the humans where not capable of understanding. you will need both the light and the Christ energy, to be able to move on to the next level of evolving. again you will learn how to communicate without words.

The Maya people knew this. Like an experiment they leveled up, years and years ago. The rest of you did not understand this because of lack of light and love in your hearts. You have always let your mind believe that the only way out of conflicts are war and only use of dark forces. You have forgotten that these dark forces are the lights twin. Without light there is no darkness and both is necessary. You need the balance. There is no evilness. The only evilness is within your hearts, because of lack of divine love. All humans will be as one. You must learn to use the light in appropriate ways. Do not fear the dark.

Look at the Native Americans. Hear their words! Understand the meanings with your hearth. Do not interpret the words. Just feel the fragrance. Feel the vibrations of the words and their singing. The drums will activate parts of your cells, that have forgotten how to use the light.

The light is in within every part of you. Remember this: In your 3D world everything has a shape and a form which you believe is the only form or shape there is to be. Like the ice cube. Due to temperature the ice cube has its form. You know that the water due to circumstances can be floating, stiff or particles in the air. Like this, shapes can shift in other dimensions, due to the power of light and thoughts.

In "our" world, as you call it, nothing or everything can take a shape or form at once you think it. Everything remembers everything. Everything is a part of everything. At the same moment you have been thinking a thought, that thought comes true at the very moment.

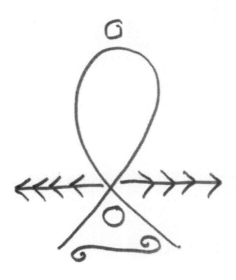

"Symbol of light"

You have forgotten how to use herbs. You have forgotten how to take care of the earth. This is why Gaia is rebirthing. This is why we are in a hurry to make this change to happen. The Universe is here to help you save yourself from not leveling up. Like Walt Disney said; "When you wish upon a star it makes no difference who you are". Just remember in your hearth. Like Peter Pan you can fly, you can reach the stars. If you believe it, achieve it and use the light.

You have been given <u>so</u> many songs. Many people have been trying to tell you our message through them. Like "Love shine a light", like "Heal the world", and the very most important the "Man in the mirror". Please be open minded. Be open hearted.

Open up for the light to get in. Let a little light shine true you. When you light up yourself, others will notice your light and wonder what there is.

What is light? Why is it important? How do I make it shine?

Speak the language of light. Feel the language of light. Speak it with your tongue. Use your hearth to create the words. You know it, you know every part it. It has always been there. There is more to come.

When you learn how to make divine love to people you hate or are scared of, like that man that caused 22th of July in Oslo. Then you are now mastering the light within. Light is love and love is all there is.

Some of you did not forget that there is more to this world than the materials and the physical body. You could not quite understand what it was so you gave it different names. You put into words different fairytales, different Gods and religions to explain what there was beyond what your eyes can see. Humans cannot speak the same language anymore. When man first tried to reach up to God, man had not experienced enough. You thought you had done it all and knew the all. The egos grew big. God saw this. In his experiment he had to create a blur in your mind to make you believe that you could not understand each other. The true meanings of the words you are speaking are hidden from you. You are separated from the source and from each other. Or so you believe.

This is Your Journey of Light

You are living in the most material time of all.

Be grateful for the rain because it is making things happen. There will be no tide wave this time. There will be a time wave. All will fall into its correct places. All time is equal. All energies does co exist. Every time is NOW. Timelines are for humankind. Wheel of time is for energy work.

3. THE LIGHTWORKER

How to be a light worker?

Humans are born with unique gifts and senses. Inside humans are glimpses of the unique unity of light and love, glimpses of The Divine. When the inner light is lit, the light helps the world becoming a better place to live. Many people undermine their inner light by hiding it. Humans are denying their own abilities and dreams. Humans denies itself. Thereby they also stop an abundance of experiences. You confirm your love by accepting yourself. Be proud of yourself! Give yourself esteem and confidence. When igniting the flame inside, you give others permission to do the same.

You learn to hide the light through your childhood and education. Different authorities urge you to be humble and to avoid showing the light. There is a purpose to distinguish those who let their inner light shine and those seeking it, only to draw attention to their own egos.

When you dare to share your light with the world, the beauty and perfection of your soul, will be clearly visible to the surroundings. You are a creature, an embodiment of your immense potentials. If your light has been kept down for a long time, it is almost invisible. Rekindle your flame!

With your heart in the driver's seat, make a list of everything that gives you pleasure and joy. Ask yourself how you in best ways can use your skills in your daily life. Gifts you are born with are conditionally given to you. Are you discovering the impact your light has on others? When you embrace your talents and share them, you are spreading light and love in the world.

Be the leader! Shine the light. Shine it for everyone. You are a light bearer. A light bearer of the North.

"Shine! Elohim Elekbah Takcha Casha Herma"
(Language of Light)

You! Be the one to shine, no one else will do it for you, so shine. Shine like the blessed star you are. Try finding someone like you, there are plenty, but well hid. Some don't even realize who they are.

The spark has not been lit. Light a spark and people will be drawn to it, like moths to a light source. It is encoded in them, as it is in you. Through though times, you have realized who you are. Your beliefs are your truth. Do not doubt yourself. How can an answer that comes from your heart be wrong? It comes from you. Directly from you. In your higher self lies your answers. You have them all, deep inside you. In your heart of hearts. Listen to the whisper of truth. Your direct connection with it all will help you, just listen. Pay attention. Forget the world outside. The others may not know you. You will always be the bearer of your own truth. Believe. Go in peace. Remember to listen and to shine. Project loved One, your heart is big enough!

You are a guide and a light carrier. You will all speak our language and tell our story, until the day your time is out! Let the tears flow and use them as a way to let the barriers down. It is time to shine and to glow with your light of divine love.

Everyone is worthy of being light workers. When you realize your full potential, you allow yourselves to be the one you were meant to be. Then you are a true light worker. Only then you will be able to use the gifts you are given. Be the light bearer. Be the force within. Use your light working productions to create and evolve.

Use your skills as a healer from Atlantic times. Heal the wounds. Free yourself from disbeliefs. Stay up and stay front. Be the light bearer to whom you were born to be. You are the light from North, from ancient times, from the beginning of time. In the beginning of time there was only light. There is no beginning and no end. Take care of your world, because you have been given a once in a lifetime chance to set things right. Not in 10 years, not in 20 years. Act NOW.

Through darkness you see light. You are a light bearer. Your DNA console is changing. Feel the change. Notice that your body is changing. Do not suppress yourself. Allow yourself to blossom. This is the only way to be the light carrier. Discover your role, do not hide.

> *"Elohim, Elohim Belek*
> *The light is always with you*
> *Oh thelek athan hem*
> *Oh thelek athan hem*
> *Oyle Oyle Oyle."*
> *(Language of light)*

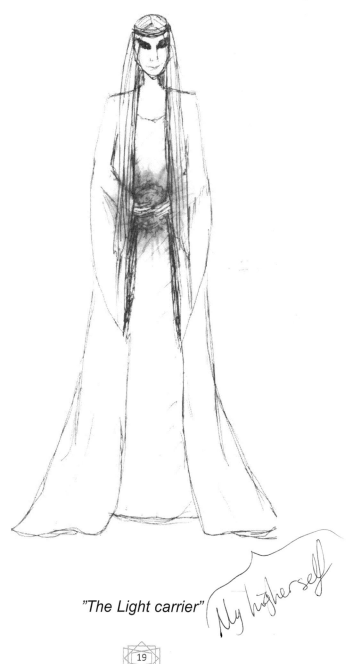

"The Light carrier"   My higherself

The Light Carrier

In the depths of your souls the light is strong. In the deep of the soul a quiet flame is glow burning. The flame is infinite. Burning intensely and quietly within. Sometimes with a sore glow. The light is your gift. Light is your life partner. The light is everything. "There's something about you", you may have heard. "It's something with your eyes. It's just as if I know you. Why? They recognize themselves in you. Your light is their light. You remind them of who they are.

Tears on the cheek. Tears like diamonds. Tears, beautiful and sorrowful. Memories of lost time. Memories of all that is. Resembles of what that comes. Love is the light source. Love is the fire of life. Grief is its sister. Let the light shine. Know your inner power. Be the light bearer and shine for yourself and others!

Namaste.

"The symbol of the light carrier"

How to live with the light

"The road to the light can often seem dark. Road going forward can often seem as though it goes back". Tao Te Ching, spiritual text.

People with extrasensory senses, often lack knowledge and confidence in what this is. You might not know how to use this senses. Often you are experiencing the feeling of being unusual that they are unusual and different. To be born with a 6'Th sense can be difficult to handle. The 6'Th sense is the senses of hearing, seeing, knowing, or feeling the energies that are located in other dimensions and frequencies. The feeling of falling outside defined frames, often contributes to depression, lack of vitality and ability to adapt to society. It has been difficult for the people through the ages to know where to turn for answers and help with questions about this topic. Often it is scary to be put in the context of spirituality or alternative society. Often human's own experiences of extra sensory perception collide, with faiths and beliefs that are learned through society. This is the story of mankind. Over perception has been regarded as an abnormality among mankind. Because mankind has developed this way of perceiving the sixth sense, the humans look at themselves as abnormal.

The key to live well with your senses is to build up confidence and awareness about what it is. You need to learn how to use your abilities appropriately. Negative reactions are only a result of a fear-based reaction that lies deep in your inherited genes. One of the many definitions of fear is "false evidence appearing real". The light within provides safety, joy and love. The light is your guide in living with 6'Th senses. The light connects the earthly "I" to the psychological higher self and also to the universal energy that everything is part of. The task is to find the creative keys which each individual has within. You have a toolbox within that will help you mastering your own life. You need to excel, to be superior, to surpass, outdo, to do better than, to experience the feeling of sovereignty.

"Learn to excel like you have been born to, by finding the light within."

By using the acknowledgement of your light and senses, you throw light over the globe. Use the light to help Earths rebirthing process ahead.

"When you let your inner light shine, you give other people the right to do the same thing"
(Nelson Mandela)

Fight your own battle

You might think differently or feel different from others. Stay focused on your own individuality. Dare to express your own uniqueness. If others are having a hard time accepting who you are, or adjust to whom you really are, you will always be the one to allow yourself to shine your light despite other meanings.

You are the only one who can find your inner light. You are the only one who can take it back. Relight the flame inside. Connect to Yourself!

To find your way back to your inner flame, the first thing you need to do, is to believe and acknowledge that there is a light in yourself. Your light source, your flash. This is the sparkle of your life!.

"Be visible in the light"

The Northern light, a meditation

Sit or lay in a comfortable position. Check that nothing is too tight on your body. Make sure your spine is straight. Make sure that the air can flow freely through the nose and down into the lungs.

Close your eyes when you're ready. Continue to breathe in a pace that is quiet and comfortable for you. Feel free to count to five while you inhale, new five while holding your breath, and new five when you exhale. Remember that your breath is your companion. It is your life mate and it will guide you through any situation in life. Just allow it to do so. Take care of your friendship within.

Continue to breathe calmly. While doing so, notice how the surface feels against your body. Feel how you, every time you exhale, are relaxing more and more. Imagine that you are being surrounded by light, by dancing lights from the Aurora Borealis. Feel how the light dances with you, how it embraces you.

Everything is in the light. Light is everywhere you are. Light is life's energy. For a while, notice now, what light shows you. It might tell you something, maybe you see something, or maybe you feel something. So for a while, let it seduce you.

(Quiet moment).

So, what is light showing you? Keep your mind still for a while. While doing so, focus on your breath. Begin to notice your surroundings, move your fingers and toes slowly. Be aware of that you are in your body. Open your eyes and be fully back in yourself. Drink lots of water. Write down your experience.

"Teveltunet, Norway, August 2011

4. HOW TO REACH THE LIGHT

How can you reach the light within that may seem to be hidden for your inner self? Would you like to search? Do you really want a change in your life?

Your inner light will lead to major changes in your life. It will lift you up to new heights and it will help you to see life in new perspectives. Would you like to search for the light within?

The light is asleep and waits for the code to open the coffin lid. This is your own treasure Chamber. You are holding the key. The wait is over! Ignite the lamp and open your soul! With your eyes closed and with wind in your hair, with water who works its way across the country, you will overcome many obstacles on your way!

Your own will

In order to reach the high frequency of your crown chakra, your own will must be present. The will to reach new heights, where unknown landscapes and unploughed mark is waiting for you, are important.

You will grow and get the nutrients that are necessary to achieve success in your earthly life. Search within with open eyes. See yourself with new eyes! Enjoy the small things of life! Make changes NOW! A burning desire is given you! A desire for everyone to take part in your world, your wisdom, your willingness to change everything that is deadlocked!

Help others to raise their eyes! Make human life something loving, something special that raises everything up and forward. Provide love for the rest of your earthly life!

Let the river fizz, let the birds chirp, let trees speak their honored languages! Listen, listen to everything that is, all is NOW!! Some listen with their inner ear. Some feel their inner light. Some bears the old wisdom with dignity. What is written in the old diary that your soul has authored? Dare you join us for the journey, to the ancient writings that are waiting?

"Ethereal food for light bodies"

Diet for a light worker

I am Amin! My earthly kingdom disappeared decades ago. All our thoughts are stored in the universal eteric field. The tracks of eteric information are open for you. Awaken channels in the DNA of people that are selected to be our messengers. The time predicts large earthly changes towards 2013. The earth's crust will move further and there will be new animal species, while others die out.

People should change their diet. Energy flows more easily when you avoid lots of chemical protein and other chemical additives. Chemical protein is protein that has turned unclean by the manufacturing process. Changes are made to the structure. Important substances are removed and unbreakable crystals occur. All additives that are artificially produced are difficult for humans or the Earth to break down. Therefore the small gray people are among you. They are cleaning up mechanical garbage. The light body you get with the changes in the DNA will need food that is made on open fire.

Homo sapiens turns into homo illuminate. Flames do not change the original frequency in food. Food made on electric hot plates destroys the frequency of food by its radiation. Light bodies are less tolerable for artificial additives as these create blocks and imbalance of the chakra points. It also contributes to disrupt the energy flow in the light body. This gives room for diseases.

Sugar was used by the Atlantic people as stimuli. It created euphorically enjoyment and experiences. It was only the initiated ones who used white sugar. They used it with caution, because white sugar in large amounts interferes with the balance of forces in brain two half's, so that the contact is disrupted and further separation occurs. Sugar in small amounts of pure light bodies seems like revelations used correctly. Other artificial sweetener hurts the light body. Cane sugar was used and can be used in small quantities. Unproccesed salt is also good for light body. More information about this will come when we will give you information about etheric cooking.

People will live shorter. The perspective of time on Earth will change. Hours, minutes and seconds will have new meanings. Look to the wheel of time!

The Light shall be carried throughout the globe. New planets come into your universe, these will influence lights appearance on Earth!

Use your intuition and follow the light. With the right intention. Intention, harmony and love for all creatures in the world! Learn from nature! Use the resources that exist in a loving way! You are the light bearer. You are light!

Keep focus

A lot of new ground-breaking information is to be found in our writings. The Council of Elders reads and interprets the symbols. Soon you will do the same. This is important for the shift of the planet. There is war among the earth people. Many people are struggling to master the changes happening in their unconsciousness. Enormous energy waves, as memory pressure from Atlantis, is now about to reach the Earth's crust!

I ask you all. Focus on the good purpose! Dear children! Locate your curiosity and focus. Light lines will lead to your correct expression! A lot of expressions from humans are from positive sources. Please be aware! New star formations are approaching. The sky is the first landing place. Get information from the etheric rays. They are here to give information to the light bearers.

Light particles and crossroads

Light particles have different charge. In order to be able to distinguish between the different depths of the raw material of information. All carry their own story! Star kids will be born with this wisdom in a micro chip. These children's choices at the crossroads are important! Crossroads are the perspective between the light and reality. Like light seen through a big diamond. Star kids are born with no hint of negative influence. They are easy learners. At the same time they are full of ancient wisdom. Learn to master the world! Many of star children will be twins.

"Listen to the light that's growing inside you!" The light carries a lot of wisdom. The old wiccans new about our mission! The mission about the light travel across the earth lines, to help the light into the new beginning! The beginning of the new era, the era of stars! "

The space in between light and reality is the place where all dimensions are.

Forgotten wisdom will reoccur

In an endless time where everything was light, a new world was born. A world that was going to be a creation of light and darkness. A Flash of rays from the Galaxy was sent to the new world.

Dolphins had their own Government where energetic sound and light rays managed communication between them.

The forgotten wisdom about this Kingdom will be resurrected! Your world is turning! You will walk in a new direction, into a new era. This is the time where your inner emotional life of light will guide you in the right direction. Relight your flame. Join us for the journey, the journey back to retrieve old wisdom and new life.

Mother Earth is struggling with the negative vibrations that are surrounding her. The negative layers are the result of mankind's negative thinking. Mother Earth needs the light from the North in order be free and newborn. Many of the answers needed to achieve this essential miracle that is necessary for the further existence, are written in the books of Destination Star 15

The stars will tell you the true story, the story about our own light. The light makes you breathe and live in peace!

Let your inner journey be the start of something new. It will open new doors and it will fill the diary of your soul with life wisdom. New chapters will be written, and new mountains will be climbed. Stretch yourself to the clouds! Accept the compliments! Listen to your inner self! Get the road that is paved and is waiting for you! Your innate life wisdom will guide you on your tour. The window to the future is open! Grab the chance!

Affirmation to get in touch with the light:

I love life and light.
Light loves me!
I see that I am a part of everything on Earth.
I am a portion of everything in the universe!
I am a unique piece in the store!
Everything I do has meaning!
The more contact I have with the light,
the more I get meaningfulness in my life!

Use this affirmation on a daily basis to create roads in yourself, so that the light appears. By daily repetition creates the recollection and awakes the light in each cell of your body and prepare it to receive light and love.

"Find your inner light"

5 ELEMENTS OF THE LIGHT

The Thoughts

Once upon a time there was a thought, a thought of light. It did not understand, and did not appreciate what it was and what it was capable of. Due to the experiment, the thought divided and suddenly there was darkness. Like Abrahams sons who were born to let you experience what happens, when you forget that you are made of the same substance. Therefore there is Allah, Jahve, God and Buddha among others.

There is a harmony between different thoughts. One person can speak Hebrew, another can translate and a third gets the message. This happens because the beliefs beyond the thoughts are equal. In ancient times, you needed no words. In your time, the words are confusing humankind. When the thoughts have been thought they are revealed for all. There was no need for words.

Once a thought came free. It divided and created another goal.

All is equal time. All thoughts are leading to the same goal, although the thought itself has forgotten. Suddenly it all came out of control, or so it seems. Not all thoughts did forget. Some thoughts did remember where they came from. Therefore the goals are equal.

You believe that Moses got the Realms from God. How can you then not believe, that there are and will be visiting energies from other planets? Because thoughts have learned you so. Thoughts are equal.

Your body is responding and remembering what the brain does not get. Get to know your symbols. Now there is equal time, it is all there is. Trust your inner light. Learn to understand the symbols. You need your thoughts like a car needs fuel. Sometimes the fuel is good sometimes the fuel is bad. You need good thoughts, as fuel, to evolve and to stay healthy.

Moses in
the fall "Brudesløret", Norway

The Ego

Your ego is standing in your way. You need your ego. You need to tame the ego in order to see the light and to feel the light. You need the ego to survive among the others. Mankind has forgotten what is behind all thoughts, all the images and all there is. It is like this: When the body is suffering, the body speaks to the mind and tells the mind that the pain is a reminder of something that is not right in the humankind life.

The ego has free will and can choose whatever it likes.

All is a state of mind. All is dependent of your thinking. Your thoughts are running true your body. They create physical feelings along their way. This is a kind of "stop and listen" sign. Your body will change because your DNA is changing.

The Balance

It is all about balance. The body speaks your mind. There is a special place in your mind .You need to reach this place through another canal. It will awake you when you are not sleeping. Listen my child - listen! This word will be the turning point in your life! Let all of the past that hurt you and made you feel small go - let it flow with the wind and help you to understand the difference between your own life and others!

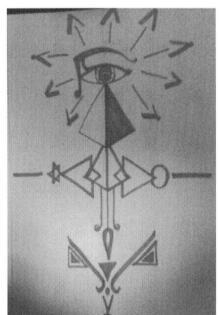

"Symbol of DNA
changes in
human body"

Image I have channeled and drawn.

Rhythm

Rhythm is important! The rhythm of breath, wind, water and speaking! Remember the life of nature. The life to come. The little things in life, the small particles. The small particles of light that you see like glimpses in the corner of your eye, the small lights that you find hard to explain. These small energy lights contain important information. Please note! You must find the rhythm! Here there is a lot to retrieve. The rhythm and melody. Use gestures. You are water, water has a rhythm, and water has a vibration.

Breathe

Inhale the light! Exhale the love you feel inside! You have to work on this. This need practice to do! You really need to feel the light and the breath, within every part of your body. You have to want this. If you don't, the information that lies between will pass you by!

Big steps are coming in your way, dear listener. Breath with your soul, it has its own rhythm, follow it! Relax and let all the noise go. Your own frequency matters! You are reaching for the stars, for the new beginning of the new world. The new people, who will be born into this circle of light, will feel divine love for all living energy. Reach your hand up to the sky and follow your heart! Listen to what really matters to you! Let all of the other information go back to the light!

Love

The base quality in humans time/space reality is love. How to stay centered means to recall balance within. It involves removing the resistance that lies within. The resistance prevents you from being your true self.

Love and light is what humans are made of. All is connected through the power of unity and love. People, who have had near death experiences, have told the world that they got a distinct feeling of being made of divine love. When they met their loved ones at "the other side", they realized that all is pure and unconditional love. The other side is filled with pure love and pure light.

Humans have many different angels to explain what love means. This is natural because humans live different lives and have had various past lives. Some have more resistance within than others. The individuals must work with various obstacles on their way to the light. The beautiful fact is that people are individuals with different perspectives. This gives them many different perspectives, different possibilities and many angels to see and understand the greater aspects of truth in the end, the image will be complete for every single one of you. The Earth has some exciting months ahead. Let us break through any form of cage or resistance and awaken to our fullest potential!

The weapon of Love

The Light of the North is shining. The Light of the North is brightening. It is here and it is strong, stronger than you think. Through fire and ice, through thick and thin they have fought. They have fought for justice with the greatest weapon: The weapon of love. Showing to the world a shining of light.

The Northern Light is important. It is wonderful and strong. Full of love it cherishes everything. You may think that it is being oblivion and too caring. The light is really showing the way. The way forward. The Northern light is before its time. It is leading a whole country through tough times like this and still it is showing love, shining its light. Huge masses of loving hearts show that humans on earth are a people made of love, and a people ready for the light.

The world is not a pure place anymore. It has lost its child, its inner child, its innocence. The light will purify it. It will wisp away all that is dark and dingy. Everything that has gone wrong will be corrected by the greatest power of all, LOVE. LOVE is a simple word. Still it is such a compact word: Emotions, facts, rage, humor, feelings. It could go on forever. Everything comes from and with love. Lately it has been shadowed by one of its byproducts, greed - malevolent greed. People are no longer happy with what they have. They want more and more. It is a new house, a bigger car, more money or more power. Power over a city, village, country, empire, union, power over the world? Do you not think it has gone too far now, my children? Too far gone the wrong way?

There is hope! In hope there is light. In light there is love. Love will pour down from the North. Pour down like a heavenly rainstorm. Be brave now! Accept the love that is offered to you. It is the easiest thing in the world and it is free. Forget cash and greed. Forget all that. The best thing is that is free. It is in abundance, unlimited and whoever wants it will get it. Rich or poor, big or small.

You are all the same and equally worthy of the greatest gift of all. Open your hands, your heart and your mind. Accept and you will release all tension that has infected your body, soul and heart. Accept, forgive and look forward with new eyes. Don't be afraid! Believe that love is all you need.

If everyone consciously and unconsciously has this thought, the world will heal its wounds. A new decade would approach. One filled with things we never would believe would be possible. Only if enough people can realize this and share this thought, only then will ultimate bliss be reachable.

Reaching for God-like serenity can seem unachievable. It is the easiest thing in the world. You make your world. You are essentially your God. By realizing that you are the one in control, there is no limit to what you can achieve.

Some people believe this, sadly most of them use it for the wrong purposes. Imagine if some of the world's greatest leaders would use their power to influence their people in a good manor, just imagine that. Imagine them using their powers to create something good out of pure love for love, not love for lust, lust of power to rule over people and not with them. Imagine that.

Your powers are greater than you ever have imagined. Your influence is great because you are so humble. Realize your potential! It will all lay down perfectly for you. You are a great leader, a good leader. Help lead the Light of the North down, up, out and in. Broadcast it, write it, say it, draw it, feel it. Do whatever suits you, just bring it out to the people. You lead the light like gold and copper lead electricity.

Light's only wish is to keep up divine love and to make everything divine love. Without divine love, there will be no light.

"Symbol of divine light of love"

Divine Love is the Key

In the beginning there was light. The lights twin was darkness. To understand itself "The All" had to create the opposite of divineness. To gain super consciousness you need to feel and to give divine love. The Armageddon of Atlantis was caused by lack of understanding, and will to see the bigger picture.

Divine Love is the key. Massive positive thoughts of divine love and forgiveness will change Abraham, Sarah, their feelings and their actions as well. I am Jesus Christ, I am here to support you, like I did then. See me like I see you. I am You, You are me. I am Maria Magdalena. Use my love, feel my love, breath love and make love divine. You where there, when there was only light.

Light and Water

Seeing beyond words is all there is. Life will be different and the Light language will be learned,

learned by all. Your stories will be rewritten. Your learning skills will be new. All comes from within.

In our spheres we do not use words like you do. It's not because we can't, it is because we have more efficient ways of communication, through the light. You have evolved differently than us. Because of this your ways and our ways will be different despite the fact that all is happening in real time.

Are you noticing shadow people in your bedroom at night? They are your students from times past and present. From Egypt, Atlantis and from the light source. As you have taught them their ways, they now watch you teaching your temporary new self how to re-establish contact with the higher you. They are there to supervise and experience your ultimate learning task, as that is what this life is all about. You are here to learn how to make life shine. Take back your knowledge as a statement of what not to make the new world like. You alone shall remember this, in order to keep other from not remembering and falling into old pathways. It's a burden to bear. This is what you have chosen to do.

Water is the purest thing that is still is to be found on earth. It has been there always, in one form or another. Because of its ability to change and adapt, it has been allowed by human kind to stay as it is for so long. Like crystals can store information on a higher frequency, the water can do the same. But on more levels, as it can change from ice crystals to humid damp to running water. Water is also a huge part of a human body and because the water has flown through all humans and animals trough time, it has traces of everything in it. All the history of time is stored within the water.

You can read the water by appreciating it, by drinking it, by bathing in it. By exchanging yourself for the water to pass through, the water will leave you information and let you interconnect with it, as it is flowing through your system. It may be hard to understand this. By being ONE with the water, you will tap into its wavelength, and gain information and wisdom.

"A single drop of water makes the biggest ripple effects"

The ice cube

The difference between yours and mine dimension is like this: In your dimension everything is like the ice cube. Water stuck in a shape. In my world it is like this: Without temperature the energy of water can have any form or no form at all. That is the main difference between your world and mine.

Trees

Trees for example, are holders of old wisdom and knowledge. Old trees that have roots going deep into the soil, hold old wisdom. But yet again, their wisdom comes from the water and the light.

Dolphins

Dolphins are a rare species and old souls. They are supernatural, although you may think that they are a creature like any other. They hold knowledge so sacred, that only the ones that now the answer and want to know will be able to tap into it. They are so much more than what people think.

They are playful souls, just do not mistake their happiness, because they sit on some deep dark secrets of mankind that should stay hidden, so only ask for what will give you joy, happiness and benefit in your life. I'm the Dolphin man, high priest of the sea. Some called me Neptune, but I am the origins of the water in a more solid form. I placed and gave the water the ability to withhold energy and information.

"The Dolphin spirit"

Gratitude

Feel gratitude for life! Imagine that you see planet Earth from space. Let it slowly come closer to you. Feel the gratitude in your heart for all the planet holds! Gratitude is love's sister.

Darkness and Despair

Light leaded to darkness and darkness leaded to shadows. The darkness exists to show you the light and give you this experience of how it feels without love and divine love. Learn to love the light, learn to love the darkness. There is no in between. There is only oneness. Look at the goddess Athena. Look at the orphans she saved with love which came from the light. Look at the stars and see how she lit their inner flame.

Humans have forgotten. Therefore they are walking in darkness and despair. Illusion is the feeling of being separated from divine love and the source.

You need to teach the people how to live and love with their abilities, that humankind has named the 6th sense.

Once we were all ONE on this planet. Now the planet is suffering in big crisis. You are sent to bring light and love back to the space between earth and sky. The DNA will swing up to a new level this fall. Stay together and use your life experiences to teach people out there about energy food and energy medication for the inner self.

You will change! You have a great gift! We will teach you how to use it the best way. All you have to do is listen! Listen carefully and be loaded with love and peace! We will fill up your cup of wisdom. You are walking at the same energy frequency and you have known each other for millions of ages. Teach the youngsters, the young adults and the adults that still have their inner child, how to be the light carriers that they truly are.

Meditation: create a friendship with your pain

This is a meditation that will help you to accept and give love to the pain in your life.

Sit or lay in a comfortable position suitable for you. Make sure nothing is too tight on your body. Breathe calm in a pace that is comfortable for you. While you do this, close your eyes and know that you are more and more peaceful for each breath. When you feel that your body is relaxing, you do envisage, or know the pain that you want to be friend. What does the pain symbolize for you, why do you have it? What do you want? Accept the information given to you by the pain and embrace it. Carry the pain into your inner light. Embrace it with rays of love, let your tears fall. Let the breath fully guide you through the process. Let the pain be part of your love. Let go of the pain.

Let light and love guide you back to now. Be aware of your body, start moving the fingers and toes. Open your eyes slowly and stay in your body. Sit up slowly up, drink a lot of fresh water, and write down your experiences.

"What is your personal Stonehenge?"

Liberation

Light creates darkness. Darkness is not experienced as darkness if you haven not seen the light. Without light darkness is not experienced as darkness. Light and dark embraces each other and makes no difference. Free yourself in every moment, loosen all thoughts and observe the thinker. What do you see in yourself? See infinity inwards, where all the wisdom and love lies. Do not look to others, look into yourself. Be the butterfly that breaks free from it's catapilar. Spread your wings, let the love shine and become your greatest potential.

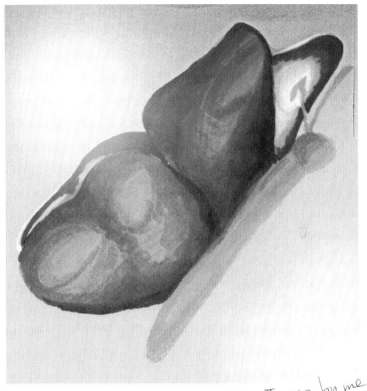

"Come fly with me" ℐmage by me!

"You have to walk your own miles and learn to trust your inner guidance to be the light carrier "

Information

If information resonates with you, it is meant for you. If it does not feel right for you, it is not meant for you. Every message that is given, creates harmony in some way with feelings inside of you. You can learn from the message and in that way the message is meant for you. Learn from it and feel what the message means for you. This is all that matters.

Change and accept

You need belief, you need faith and you need healing. It is like when you are getting new shoes and their hurting your feet. Then your thoughts are all circling about the feet area of the body, and you now you have to change something to feel well. It is like this. You all need your comfort zone, and you all need to get out of the comfort zone. Then you will experience things that don't feel good. Then you need to change.

Have a good state of mind, body and soul. Feel good no matter where you are. Do you need the comfort zone? You need your body and mind to feel safe and aligned, wherever you are. May the entire universe and time and space be your comfort zone.

Do not feel guilty if you find it hard to manage to change the course. Sometimes the meanings of why things are in such state are hidden for you. There are limits to the human brain. You need fait, trust and healing to stay positive and open minded. Use the light to be free and use the light to be well.

Change always hurts because you are human.

Sometimes changes are in need of big amounts of will, luck and pain. This is because you are earth bound. Changes do not happen in a snap. Keep your attentions to all positive things or happenings in life. Have faith that all will be good.

Language of Light

Language of light is different than other languages. It is an activation language used several times in history. Its purpose is to create a conscious change, to the people that are willing to make the shift happen. The language of light has no alphabet. The sounds and the symbols are the essence of knowledge. In this book we have guided you to write Language of Light with your alphabet in order to reach out to you that yet do not know the meaning of the symbols.

People are no hunters. They are teachers sent to the earth to stay as a barrier! The eagle will come back and create a vision of lost life and lost wisdom.

"Eykeleh ey ey ey aheylek aheylek a heyle,
The eagle is the symbol,
Okaa le ey ey ey akyle ! Eheyleke he hem akeyla"
(Language of Light)

The roses

Many people say that life is not a bed of roses. However, it is? Roses are beautiful. Roses are in many colors. They need nourishment. Roses have thorns. Roses grow and die, and are bearers of a set of wisdom. People create bouquets of Roses, as they do with their memories. The humans plant roses in pots, mirroring their own life living in houses. Humans have roses in their gardens as a memory of their own freedom in nature. Humans take care of the roses where ever they have them, as a reminder of that humans should take care of each other and their environment.

Human life goes in circles just like the life of roses. They are born, they grow, they learn, they need nourishment and love. And finally their earthly body dies. Every human has a relationship to roses. Who has not got stung by them? Just like the human life, every now and then humans bump into something hard that gives them a new experience "the hard way".

There's a lot of wisdom hidden in Roses, just like in man himself. Listen to see what's hidden! Adapt a child's curiosity. Immerse yourself in this parallel life you're living with roses. Locate the power and the essence of each branch and leaf, just like yourself. Search the knowledge that resides and waits for you! Maybe you're a Rose Bud? A bud that is about to break out in full bloom? Perhaps you ignore the signals given you, so the experience passes? Be sure that you get to know all the beautifulness there is!

Experience the scent of the roses. Take part in their wonderful world of new and fresh wisdom! No fight against yourself is simple. The only certain thing is that everything certainly changes and that humankind attends a lifelong school of life full of experiences and knowledge. It needs a little resistance in order to determine your highest potential. Perhaps the human appreciates the light more, when the storm has settled? The light you carry within you, is necessary for your inner journey to your own treasure Chamber. The Chamber that contains all the wisdom from all your life, and all the lessons learned through thousands of years. Lit the flame! Take the chance! A barrier needs to be broken. New steps must be taken. A new way of viewing life is arising.

Rose garden, a meditation

Feel that you are lying or sitting in a comfortable position for you. Note that the spine is straight, and feel that the air flows freely and undisturbed through the nose and down into the lungs. Breathe calm in a pace that is comfortable for you, feel free to count five of the inhale, while keeping the air in the lungs and again to five as you exhale. Do this a few times until you feel calm and know that your body is relaxing more and more. In doing so, as you will notice the sounds around you, know that they are pleasant and quite natural.

Continue to focus on your breath. While doing this, imagine that you are sitting in a rose garden. Surrounded by roses of all colors and all variations. Imagine that one of the Roses is your mirror. This rose represents you, look closely at it. What will it tell you? What kind of smell? How it feels to touch? How many leafs are there? Does it have a voice? Does it have a sound? Just keep this moment for a while now. Feel what the message is.

(Quiet moment)

Focus on your breath and continue to breathe in a comfortable and relaxed pace. Begin to notice that you are in your body, move slowly on fingers and toes, and open your eyes when you're ready for it.

Write down your experiences for future use.

Remember to drink lots of water, and write down your experiences.

"The Rose"

6. THE SYMBOLS AND THEIR MEANINGS

You will learn how to use the symbols and get to know their specific meanings. The symbols are for each and every one of you to understand. So you can reach each other, in the sphere beyond words. Now you have learned how it feels and what it is like to be separated from the source and from each other. You have learned to feel feelings you could not be able to understand without this experience. This knowledge is important for your understanding of the symbols.

Frequency – Sound

Symbols are portals to wisdom. There is a correlation between what human sees and what humans feel. There is a special frequency in the symbols that humans can only get through symbols. The vibration of the symbols affects the water reservoir in the body so that humans can understand wisdom through hearing. Your hearing will then be more able to perceive the higher frequencies. This is possible due to DNA development. Listen to the rhythm of the new frequencies provided for you! The high frequency of Dolphins will be leading in retaining the light's language - "The Language of Light".

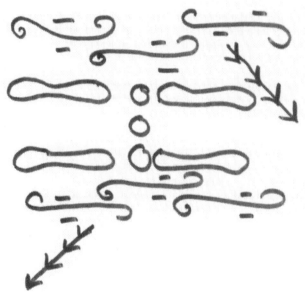

"Symbol of sound"

Your understanding comes through inner balance.
Your clear hearing will be more important than your
language! Please be punctual in your choice. Your
knowledge is not widely known. The Lady with the
black hair, want to know how the language of light
looks like! The angels, and the teachers and
guardians of the Holy Grail is there help you. The
Holy Grail and Akashic records are opened for you,
to give you understanding. Look beyond the words.

The sound of the dolphins will balance your inner
sphere. It will create peace within. A door in time for
old knowledge to again enter the light will be
opened by the dolphins. Brain frequency will allow
deeper information and differentiated dimensions to
establish contact with you. Dolphins provide
answers to questions about how to divide water. Be
ready to receive new wisdom. Water, tears of water
and salt, is the formula for crystals. Crystals give
purity. Waves and wave lengths create harmony

and open doors to the hidden wisdom of the light particles.

Water

Salt + water + light + formula for love = revelation! This formula will be given you when you are ready to understand.

Lost knowledge appears through symbols. This will cause unrest and tensions in humans. Longing, missing and grief will be redeemed! Now a new time of love begin. A new world will be revealed. Time is omnipotent. An Association of powers is going to happen. All time is at the same time. Now light creates differences in time. The illusion is complete. The structure of the rose leaves, the light of infinity and the lights shape ability, creates diversity in time. Look inwards at the flare. The answers lie within!

Hiking in the "Under water tunnel" creates a Visual break, a still image of something that is not. Currently lacks a development branch (to the left) that has not come yet. It will appear when the time is given. The symbols must be used and understood before the next level can be reached. This will not be given before the fluid is in balance, and the love frequency is in place. It will be difficult to understand for the people, when they are in need of more information. However they will recognize by going back to the symbols.

"Symbol of water"

.

Water – look at the light in the water, as an experiment to understand the different water particles. See with the inner eye, otherwise you will miss out on information. The experiment has to be done in darkness so that you may not be "deceived" by your human eyes. Shine your inner light! Image: River in the mountain, as a symbol of the fresh water! Movement is important for their understanding and ownership of the symbols. Common understanding and resonance in the unit is important.

"Symbol of earth frequency in its third power"

Meditation, "under water tunnel"

A trip to your inner treasure. Use whale song as background music.

Find a comfortable place where you can sit or lie undisturbed. Focus on the sound of music as well as your own breath. Inhale your breath deep down in the stomach, and exhale out again while counting to 5. Do it now.

Think or imagine that you're diving down in a sea of colorful fish, where corals and dolphins welcome you.

Focus on your breath, and let yourself follow the waves. Be sensitive to what you see, hear and feel!

Rest!

The waves will take you down to an opening in the corals, a door into a lighted tunnel. Notice all the gorgeous details on walls and ceilings. Feel how the energy runs through your body!

Rest!

Let the water bring you further inland in the South. At the end of the tunnel there is a chest of wisdom expecting you. It can help you with the answers to your desired insight. Repeat to yourself, your intent with this journey.

Rest!

Coffin lid opens and you will now receive a notice from your inner flame, which has been hidden from you. Accept, and feel the flame spread throughout your body!

Rest!

When you feel ready for it, return the same way you came. Through the tunnel, into the sea and up to your own world. Do this at your own pace.

Rest!

Now you can move your fingers and toes. Open your eyes when you're ready for it. Feel free to write down the message you received on your journey!

Namaste`

"The Journeys You are about to make are all yours.

All Journeys are within your own inner universe"

7. WISDOM FROM BEYOND

An amazing star, on the earth's rainbow is what you are

Times are changing - earth switches her lines, ready to rebirth. All over the world mankind is suffering. Not only from hunger and starvation caused by lack of food.

Mankind is suffering from starvation due to lack of light and love. The merging of the stars makes mankind remembers. Remember that there is something they have forgotten. A longing for somewhere, someone or something starts to groan within. Darkness separated us. Light made us. Use both, to be one again.

The longing tears mankind apart. Relationships are torn apart. Feelings of depression and a need to cry fills your heart. Life suddenly changes for no reason. Or so it seems.

Starvation of the heart makes your body sick. The energy moves slowly through your body. Emotional pain makes you pay attention to sections of your body. It speaks to you. It speaks the language of love and light. Pay attention to your body. Make your journey more pleasant by accepting. Acceptation is your key.

From this moment, let your left and right brain hemisphere work together. You need them both, do not neglect them. Let them speak to you their different languages. Let them create divine love. Let them feel the Source.

For now, integrate your brain, your body and mind as one. Build bridges within to use all your powers and all your resources.

"An amazing star on the earth's rainbow is what you are.

I'm Izrael, Destination Star 15.

"What is your rainbow color?"

Channeling done by me from my highest self.

Message from a higher self

I do know that I will return. It is a comforting thought in the back of my mind. I do miss the part of me that is you. You are me and I am you. We are meant to be one, and I miss you. Sending down a particle of my light soul, was not the easiest of decisions. Seeing what you are creating and what you are becoming makes it all worth it.

I know that you will come back when your mission is complete. It will be the reunion of all reunions. I miss you and I know you feel the same. We will be one soon. Very soon. You can feel the longing. I can see and sense that you do.

Don't worry and don't doubt your feeling of not having a bond with the earth souls. You are different. You are me. A part of me was needed now, like it was needed to teach the people of Atlantis about the power of energy and crystals. I came in person then, you came in person. Our short reunion in timelines, was as comforting and blissful for me, as it were for you.

You know you are here for a reason. You are different from the others. You look like the others. Under your shell-like exterior you are of the light and so much more, because you are me.

We can meet and speak whenever you want to, because we are one. Think of us like twins, made from one into two. The connection, the telepathy is there. In your dreams, in your head, in your words and in your mind. Remember me, because I too feel a bit lonely without you. You are my "heart light". Sent directly from my heart down to this earth. Believe, because you are a part of something great. I can see through your eyes and I know what you are feeling. Like right now I can see that you, in the corner of your eye notices, that the hand that is writing is glowing. It has an aura of white/blue light. This is your light that is coming through because you are using your connection, your power. I can hear that you are thinking that this might be your fantasy talking. What is fantasy really? Can something that comes from you be the truth, just because you are the only one experiencing it? What your left brain may think is fantasy is your other brain half's dimensional truth and reality. Which is where I am, waiting for you to come back to me. I am always here, if you need me. You know how to reach me, cause I am you. Love, shine, live. You have a chance to do something amazing now. Use it. Glow!

"I am you from another time and space. My wisdom is yours. I am of the light."

The Drums of war will fade

I am the great I am and so are you. I was sent to earth to teach the people that they are more than human bodies, they are of the source. I did give you the golden rope when you were youngsters, so that you never would forget and easily could find the way back to me. The Christ energy is needed to make all the light carriers glow, and to raise the vibration field in order to level the whole world up

The drums of war will fade; the drums of wisdom will play. We will give back what was taken! Tears will come and children will play. Give back what was taken! The smoke from the fire will leave in circles, so will the people. Sing with the moon and dance with the rain. Please give back what was taken!

You needed to experience all the hard times in order to be able to be the persons you were born to be. Strong light bearers from the north.

I am Pechama; I am the great grandfather of all times. You must gather people, to help them find their source - play the drums, speak the language and BE! I am Pechama the great eagle. I am from north, south east and west,

"Keylak eyhlana"
(language of light)

They came to teach you about life. They did not know about your past life cycles. Use the wisdom from your past life to find yourself again. You are who you think you are! A piece of you will come back to this earth when your time is out, that peace will bring a great barrier in some people's life. The wisdom will be a savior for many people. Listen to the wind, listen to the rain, and listen to the inner words that are ready to come out!

We thank you for open up your channel for this information today. We will leave you now, and come back soon. Remember you are much loved and very important for this communication!

"Ey ey ey ehekly aley
Love the earth as you own child"
(Language of light)

You need to teach the people how to live "normal" lives, and that the 6th sense or so called are a natural part of life. Gaia is rebirthing in order to gain freedom and will be set free. Free from the massive negative layer of negative energy created and generated from humankind thoughts. Listen to the destination star 15, there will be new tools given to you to succeed! Love is all there is.

Source: The Great I am, Pechama

Channeled by me!

See the world through a grain of sand.

Then build it up, sandcastle after sandcastle. Some will be ruined by the waves. As the child you are sitting at the beach. You will learn the ways of the nature once more. This time you will learn them by Mother Nature herself and the Father of the sky. These will be your parents, because you are their offspring. From the beach you will venture deeper into the landscape. There you will start building your life.

I'll stand there, shining, with my arms open to give you the tools, for your new life and world. Your tools will be in your mind. This place is like no other place, and here we don't use your ways of building. Here the life is a conscious stream of believe that builds a new reality.

A council will hold the final vote, for what it will be like. You all are creators and are creating your reality. This will be like a dream reality. It is the closest thing we can describe it to. You will be beings of higher frequency. Light, power and will and soul-vise belonging on another plane than the one you will be making. Describing it as a dream world, is the easiest way.

You can compare your present state to this state. The only difference is that you will be able to go in and out of that world. You will be conscious and fully a part of your light being. Therefore you can choose where you want to create. You will be a superior being compared to what you are now.

The council of the Iliad will oversee the new world as the new lightened souls establish themselves, to their new reality. You will be able to go away from this new world, and travel to your preferred destination. As one of the "high people", you will again be a teacher of the old wisdom. Thankful for being back where your true place is, in your true form. You will glow and glorify the worlds all over. Travelling at the speed of light, because it is all light. Going from one place to the other will be easy, like breathing air when there is air all around.

Camaguru will help you set up your old you, as you have seen a glimpse of before. He is your mentor, a father and leader of your people. Yet again, you will receive your fire ball of light and love, that will give unlimited love and light to everyone around you. You will literary be a pillar of the society.

I am Carmengadis Camaguru, high priest of the alexia's galaxy nr, 3883, Leo constellation, Carinaghi Carmengadious, mother of the winds and hope of the future. Listen to your peoples blessings, as you are on your return journey back home and to the new world. We will be waiting.

"Shaliah kanliahg ak ah jagha.
(Language of light)

Stop and look around, within, on top and below. The signs are there, and you are ready to unveil them for the rest of the world.

Source: Carmengadis Camaguru, high priest of the alexia's galaxy nr, 3883, Leo constellation,

Image by me

"

Destination Star 15

I am Ashika and I will guide you through Destination Star 15. Let me know, what is there what you would like to hear from me. What is there I shall show you? What is there for you to experience?

Decades ago, there were strings from the human heart to our frequency. Now the strings are gone, because of the lost worlds, and because of the energy fields surrounding earth, like a shield of bad energy, polluting energy.

You know us, you know me. You can feel me, Sometimes we are around you, trying to give you messages that humankind clearly not understand yet. We have given you all the symbols in the crop circles. All information lies within.

Destination star 15 is where you come from. You will also return. Like you, we are human looking and we are living in what you call paradise or the other side. Though yet to be seen. Destination Star 15, is different from what you imagine, because you have the humanly bounding and that your eyes are not able to see those higher frequencies.

"Symbol of Wisdom"

Long time ago. Some of us died, due to the water that took us all, because we did not understand the power that lied within. Therefore almost all of us died. Some people of our kind did survive and you know them. You will recognize them through their eyes. You have the common meaning of symbols and understanding. DNA frequency is the same. You are not earthlings.

Question: Is this the native people?
Answer: Yes they are.

Your society is about to collapse, your mission is to reach out and take the hands of those that have the light particles within.

Question: How do we find the people with the light particles within?
Answer: Some of them already know, and some of them will wake up reading your script. You have already awakened people.

Question: Will the people wake up by them self, reading the script?
Answer: Yes some will do that.

Question: How do we wake up the rest?

Answer: Not all are to be, you will reach out to those in need, and you will guide them and help them through the awakening. There is a time for you and that time is NOW. Watch out for their eyes.

Question: Can you tell us more about Destination Star 15?

Answer: For you we are a secret society that lives decades and galaxies away. We are the silent people. We have learned to take care of the natures interests, and to use our abilities not with the ego, but for the common, for the divine, for the one. Our mission on earth has failed several times. And several times things have happened on earth, astonishing things that you cannot explain, like Stonehenge, like the Pyramids.

Question: Did you build them?

Answer: The light builds them.

Question: But you where the constructors?

Answer: Yes a kind of. We all are constructors. Every time, information got lost due to earthlings trying to destroy everything, every piece of us, because they did not listen.

Question: Are you present here on earth among us now?

Answer: Yes we are.

Question: Where?

Answer: Right here now.

Question: Are you in a different dimension? Are you invisible? How is the presence?

Answer: Sometimes you can recognize us like people, different people. You can feel a different vibration from others. You can also find us, as glimpses of light.

Question: You have no visible bodies for us to actually see?

Answer: Sometimes you will recognize us in people. You will feel the difference in the vibration between us and other people.

Question: So you mean that you are actually born in a human body?

Answer: Some are yes. There are not many of us.

Question: Anybody here, around us?

Answer: Not like newborn. Particles from us, large amounts of particles from ancient times are among you.

Question: Who are you compared to the Arcturians?

Answer: Much the same. We are all of the same, just different types and expressions of the same. We needed to experience diversity.

Question: Are you monitoring the earth from space like the Arcturians does, to help the consciousness shift?

Answer: Yes. Speak to the dolphins, they can give you much information if you just want to listen. Keep your mind still. Just Do! Your human brain will give you difficult times because of your thinking.

Question: How is the best way to get the information that has been lost so many times? Can we get it written down?

Answer: Get connected and ask.

Question: Like we do now?

Answer: Yes

Question: You said earlier that some of the earthlings destroyed the information given to the humans. Can you please give us the first part of this information? This is so important.
Answer: The main part is that you have forgotten to connect to the light. You have forgotten how the use the water, you must use the water in order to see and to get the lost information. Your brain finds it too complicated to understand everything, that I will tell you. I will give you a picture of what I mean. Soon cars will drive only from using water. This is what you have forgotten. You have got it all wrong. You have interpreted all books all the wrong ways, you are understanding progression backwards.

Question: Could you repeat that?
Answer: You have understood progression backwards.

Question: What kind of progression?
Answer: Development, industry,

Question: You mean we are moving in the wrong direction?

Answer: So you have been for several years. All the information we gave you which got lost through the Atlantis, through the Maya people, through the Tenochtitlan's. That kind of information destroyed by the earthlings, would have helped you develop other resources. You must get free. I will leave you for now. I will come to you in your dreams, both daydreaming and dreams through the night. So pay attention and write down the pictures I give you and soon you will understand.

Question: If we want to connect to the dolphins, is there a convenient time to do so now?
Answer: You can connect to anything at anytime you want.

Question: Because there is no such thing as time?
Answer: Exactly!

Question: Why is the dolphin spirit so important?

Answer: Ask them and you will find out. I am leaving you.

Source: Ashika, Destination Star 15, Hercules family, galaxy 4783 in Corvus constellation, center of planet Nebula in The vermillion Bird of the south.

"Symbol of Destination Star 15"

Sharak – Torch bearer for the Star 15.

Star frequencies contain particles from wisdom transmitted and received by the Holy Grail. Each particle is a "book", a series of ancient beliefs and work. Our ritual will resurrect this wisdom. Our dancing with the stars will provide nourishment to a new millennium.

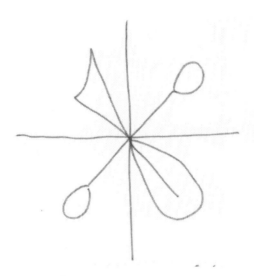

"Symbol of the holy grail"

Dear children, be true to your innate wisdom. Your inner light will be your head torch. We will send new torch bearers to you when the time is right.

You will learn how light of light will be rekindled. It will never fade out in our galaxy. Your DNA will change more and more as you are receiving our wisdom. It's necessary for you, as the channel to be adapted to our transmitter

Question: I am worthy of this task? Answer: You are selected by our Council. You and your colleagues will go on this journey towards the extent. Please be patient!

Question: What can we expect? Answer: You will receive cutting-edge information that the current science does not understand - yet. Books will be written like on a conveyor belt. Information from various sources will be crossed, and creating more sense together than separately! Each of you has your unique channel, where different info from the same sources will come

through. Put this together and the big picture will be
created.

Source: Sharak, torch carrier Destination Star 15

Imag
by me.

"Who are you?"

Meditation from "The white Eagle"

Breathe my child breathe! Raise your spirit up to the mountains and feel the sorrow that lies within.

Let the light guide you, and make you feel the healing. Your journey starts where the mountains ends! Walk, walk up to the next level of your consciousness! Listen to the song from the sea.

The Dolphins will play, the Mountains will sing, and the Eagles will bring you the new light of love!

Write down your feelings, beliefs, your goals and achievements. Do this to see how your brain is working.

"White Eagle"

The Dolphin Spirit

In the land of Lemuria the dolphins were the creators. They were in Lemuria before the people arrived. They're high frequency in life made the balance of the water. They were creators of the balance between the water life and the earth life. The animals that were first living in the water were thought to live a life on foot. The dolphins will teach you how to carry your own body and remember – you are very much water. The sensitive people, who have a lot of light particles, will learn how to make the dolphins frequency. Remember the rhythm! You people have forgotten the rhythm, the rhythm in you, the rhythm in between you and the light!

The dolphins were creators of the water balance and the light rhythm over the water. Remember they were here before you! Don't let your arrogance push them away. They can teach you! Some people have seen the dolphins as they really are. They use dolphins to heal people, to help people who need the frequency, who need the song to heal pain and to be stronger from inside and out!

The destination of star 15 knows this rhythm. They wants you to explore and find out if it's important for you to feel this on your own body, and remember the space in between your body and your light ball. All people have a giant light ball around them. I'm not talking about the aura, this is something else. A giant light ball, is the creation that can make you carry the light also in between - not only within.

Look into the eyes of a dolphin. You will see the green light. The green light particles that some people who walking on earth also have. That's the sign you need to have to recognize your own people.

Use your hands to find the small things that you can't see – you can feel! Use your fingertips to feel. Pick up a stone from the ground and feel. Close your eyes and use your other senses to find the truth inside of yourself. Use all of your chakras to live your life in balance!

The most of the people are stressful. They are walking through all they're life with only use of two chakras. The chakras on top, the rest of the body is not functioning like it should. Most people have forgotten they're old wisdom about the dolphins who were the true creators of the only real balance.

The people came to this land and they took it as their own. They forgot to listen, they forgot to feel, they forgot the wisdom that they had between and within. They treated the dolphins as fish. And remember my child – the dolphin are not a fish! They are playful, they are happy. But the people made the water an unhappy place, because of their wrong thinking. They made their own mission that took over the land that were not their own. Touch the dolphins and close your eyes and feel the vibrancies in the water and the particles that shine through their skin. Be a part of them. Let them know that you want them well! Let them know that you need their information and their old wisdom.

Image by me.

"The Dolphin Spirit"

Make a change! Make a change in your own life, as well as in other people's lives. Remember you can help some! Only some people can be helped, that's the difference between you, your inner life, and others. You have the particles that you need to understand. Feel don't think!

I can tell you about a forgotten land. A forgotten land where the dolphins were living alone in their own balance. They lived in their own frequency in their own sunshine. The people destroyed their happiness. Remember that you can make a life change. Be a part, be a part of the wisdom inside of you! The light, the light craft. Be who you are! Be yourself! Help us to breath – try! If you need us you know where to find us. We'll be here for you, any time! Thank you for listening!

Source: The Dolphin Spirit

Image by me

"The green sparkle in the eyes, the beholder of wisdom and the map to and through time"

This is my first Channeling.

You are The One You Believe!

You're anointed with a blessing, a blessing from the stars, to lead generations over the edge. Know you are not alone, for there are plenty.

Light is the way, although the road may seem dark. There is light in you, light all around. Nothing is impossible if you only believe, and believes that is crucial right now.

Lead the way, you lead the way. It is right, now is right, time has come. You came from far back. From within you are here, to cure the darkened mind with your gifts.

The light is the answer, and you are the bearer. Come now child! Human child, ancestor of the stars, soul of eternity. Lead the way for the masses.

Lighten the darkened road, because you are the one. The one and all. The all of everything.

You are supposed to be here. The light is lit, the flame is burning and you are one of the bearers. Help others to light their flame, because it is crucial that the flames glow. When they glow they glow for everyone.

No one will be alone in the sea of light. Everyone is everyone in the light, in the flame of love. We want you to come back. As easy as you were sent down, you will return. You have the call. It is important to make others hear the call, and answer it.

Believe you are important. You are a great leader. People will see your light, the light of all light, and some will understand. Some will say you are a kind person that has helped them on a material left side way. Others will look you in the eye and recognize you for what you are: A carrier of the light of truth.

You are here for a reason. You are the reason, everyone is. You are surrounded with light and love from so many angles and angels, that science will never understand.

You are the light; be the light. Forever shine. Love: Angel Gabriel, the master, the One, the light, it all, everything. Go in love and peace my child and the rest will follow you, for you are the one you believe. Shine!

Source: Gabriel, the Archangel

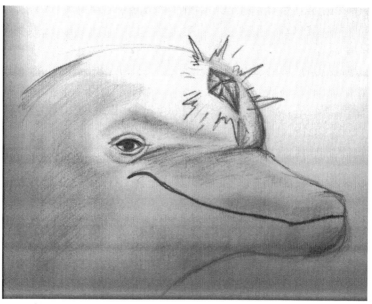

Image by me.

"The Sparkle of the Dolphins"

Sparkle of the Dolphins

I am the sparkle from the dolphins. I am a particle of the light that divides the waters. Know my knowledge, make it your own. Light blends and the light divides. Light particle on atom level, the speed of light is an illusion. As the tunnel by the transition, as portal by its destruction.

The light's power in my vibration, wave frequencies of light and sound. Which for you are separate, and for me is the same. The ones that are mastering division of water, have truly understood the meaning of the symbols. The stones will be revealed, the symbols will explain the inscription on the stones. I am the sparkle from the dolphins. A glimpse from the time you have forgotten.

The atoms of the light, will repeal gravity. Use of light atoms and water energy in the individual's particle structure, will safeguard the structures, despite the changes made. The grain is not getting destroyed by the heavy rain. However, the grain gets destroyed if the light does not take darkness away. You see with eyes which do not understand. You see beautifulness. Look behind this and see the true meaning of it. You need to calm down your thoughts. Do not let fear rule. You must get balance on all levels. Get balance between light and water.

It's like a tempest in every man, where time spins faster and faster around. Where feelings become stronger and stronger and more pronounced. The reactions are clearer. The picture of the world will be easier to understand, yet more chaotic to read. This is the signs before the stones reappear.

The way you look at the world depends on where you are. It is like a ball of yarn. Do you see the world inside and out or outside and in? Do you see how the threads are wound into a whole? Or do you only see the different threads of yarn as a net around you? Please note the perspective angle, please note how light falls from where you stand. The most glories is to fall, the biggest shall fall. With symbols you can protect yourselves.

Seid-man[1], who almost killed the Earth, can return. Do not be afraid, your strength is greater. Feel free to use it. Be careful and use it when appropriate. Do not waste it on inter-human negativity. Be ready accept all here is. The power of the symbol is your brand. (During playback of the recorded sequences, a low and a high sound occur.)

Question: You refer to Seid man who almost killed the Earth. Who is this man, what kind of energy is it?

Answer: In these days he is disguised. In these days he seems good. He knew the power and he used it to subdue and kill people. He misunderstood the symbol's meaning. This was his doom. It was his experience and it was your experience on Earth. There is no family after this man. He didn't know what love was. He received visions. He put reality in wrong timeline. His cruelty is a mirror of the infinite love he felt.

Question: Do you have a name?
Answer: Alfred was his name.

---

[1] The seid-man is well known in Scandinavian mythology. The seid-man was a wiccan.

Question: Hitler?

Answer: That was his father's name.

Question: How can we recognize him on Earth? You say he is disguised?

Answer: If you listen to your heart you will know. If you use your common sense you will believe he is the Savior. Not like the Christ energy was intended. You will find the signs, but it does not matter. Concentrate on the light.

Question: You refer to divide the water. Can you say something more about what lies behind this?
Answer: By dividing water molecules you preserve the light and the changed structures do no harm. By changing the water energy frequency, you do the impossible possible, seen from a human perspective.

Question: Are we talking about changing the energies then?

Answer: By splitting the water energy arises. This is a channeled energy, an etheric energy. The energy is tip and narrow. By dividing the water, the water is cleaned. By doing so you also cleanse the waters surroundings. It's redemption of tears. Use a microscope. Know your knowledge. Use it. Do not fear. The Angels are standing around you as a screen against your own thoughts and against others thoughts and reactions. Feel within that you are ready. You are ready for it. You have passed their school. The first step has been completed. Find your Tabernacle. Put your hand at the Holy Grail, that forever will unite. The golden energy, the clear light, the infinite love.

Question: Where do we find the Holy Grail? Answer: Until the stones are revealed, it will be hidden to others. For your inner vision, it will be available. Lift your hand in the air, and you will know it, it's here now. As a hologram, as a metaphor, as a hologram you can feel, smell and see. It's the source of life. You are guardians, caretakers. The time has come for the shift to be implemented. Let it happen.

Question: When will the stones be visible again? Answer: "Elachim ehneyh Elachim ehneyh eheynak a. Akahey eym". Seek and you shall find.

Question: Can you translate for us? Answer: (silence) This DNA is changing. Take care of the children to come.

Question: The language that came, is it the Language of Light or Hebrew?

Answer: They are not separate. Hiburu is the ancient language, before the time of the alphabet. Crystals and stars, symbols, and images where everything was more vivid than described. Search for answers in hieroglyphics.

"Wisdom from Nefertiti"

Wisdom from Nefertiti

See the Sun and the molecules against each other. See the Galaxy as a DNA string. On the road to your inner light you will experience physical changes and you will experience mental reactions. This is caused by adjustment, transformation of the individual cell and activation of DNA that has been in hibernation for many years. You can feel it difficult to use your eyes, as you are accustomed to using them, you can see things you think you do not see. You can get pixel vision, or 2D vision. Or all of a sudden, see things in other dimensions, that you do have not seen before. Some humans get sudden awakenings, while others receive a gradual adaption.

Search within Enoch's lost books. Find the answers you are missing. There are several excluded books that contains documentation, and source evidence of the Holy grails role. To use your inner light, just take small steps, keep the focus on yourself and how you're inner light affects those around you. If you start to use your inner light of selfish reasons, it will no longer benefit you. Be aware of what the starting point for your needs is.

The triangles

The two triangles illuminate each other. Place them in multidimensional forms. You will then see how all time is equal. The light shining through the triangles inter tangled, creates the feeling of a different time.

Use your heart as the sender for your thoughts. Let your mind rest. Every awakening is a gift. It is always so. A gift creates envy. Human beings are governed by their ego. Therefore, envy is a natural reaction and nothing to fear.

You shall not make the portal so narrow that no one in the great mass can pass. Then you will not see the unity needed, to lift the Earth up. Elite people that blocks out masses of its mission will not succeed. Make the light, the wisdom and the divine love available to the masses. It is not reserved a few of you selected. All are selected. It's like the wheels of a car. It is very difficult to move your car if a wheel is not functioning. The car is not able to move out of its own power when a wheel is missing. Excluding the masses is like damaging a wheel.

Question: How do we make it easily available for the masses, who basically are not very interested in this topic?

Answer: Everyone has at some point in life been somewhat interested in this subject, in terms of science, history, archaeology, computer games or movies. It's just not enough to create a casting spoon, to form the unique people to a unity. Those who try this have misunderstood, what it means to be a unit. The unity is diverse. The unity is not an entity, if not diversity occurs. The way you can reach out to the masses, is to make the wisdom available in a casual language. However, it should still be paid for, to be treasured by the masses. The price should be at a level that it is reachable. People must learn themselves how to use this tool of light. You must give them the admission ticket. So they can choose which way they want to follow.

Question: Should light workers travel around to hold lectures and similar activities to awaken the masses?

Answer: This can be done when the writing is done. When it will be possible, it will be as it should be. Lectures and instruction, but easily available and not to narrow.

There are many people out there who have an inner sadness, an inner unresolved pain. They feel sick. They can't find their place in society, no matter how much they try. This is the light workers, who not yet understand their role and does not see their place in the big picture. It is important that you reach these people with your message. The more people you are, the easier the shift will be.

There are so-called alien among you. It has done since dawn. These are hybrids and are of you as well. They are here to remind you of the work you are going to do. They will give you back the lost knowledge. Look for the pillars at the entrance to Atlantis, look for the traces and the answers in Egypt, which has not been resolved by humans yet.

Do not be afraid. Fear is created by ego. Love is universal and is in everything and everyone.

" Let your inner light sparkle, get rid of the shell"

Atlantis

Once upon a time the world looked different. Long time ago Atlantis was to be seen in the Atlantic Ocean. It was a continent that got lost when Mother earth suffered from accidents. Accidents that were created by people that used the power the wrong way. Someone is misusing the power today as well. There is a connection between the Atlantic people, Egyptians, Indians in the Americas and Mexico. You can find the remains of lost science all over the world. Look in Norwegian Viking history as well. If you look past the words, that have been used at any time. Look at the symbols, you will understand what you can't express in words. Excavations in Egypt were kept hidden, because of earthlings who fears that a change are to take place. And they fear that lost knowledge shall come forth again. This again makes it unnecessary, to use money and power to survive.

Wall Street and 11.11.11.

The movement that started on Wall Street is one of the signs before the stones again appear. There is no defined leader. The masses are wakening up to know, that they are part of a whole, which is not defined by money or power. These people are true light workers. The masses will arouse because they know within, that there is knowledge that is hidden by the naked eye. Because humans are brainwashed by all the hidden propaganda, that makes people forget where they come from and where to go. There is no danger in watching TV, reading newspapers and listening to radio, when it happens consciously. You know that you may be affected and therefore will forget. The day where the energy is taken out of the air and converted into what people need to live, as it once was. Then the shift has taken place. Earthlings are falling off, while humankind moves on with the Earth in the new dimension. And it will no longer be a threat. The

11.11.2011 represents the Holy Trinity. This date will be felt by some. It is up to the man himself.

"Learn your symbols"

Keywords to understand the light

❖ Dishonesty and manipulation of yourself: This increases the distance to the light.

❖ Learned ways to cover up feelings, stand up as something other than you are, has to be scraped away to be a light worker.

❖ Awakening: To be honest and sincere to yourself.

❖ Orion's belt – the pyramids of Giza-> DNA – reveals the wisdom that for people yet are hidden.

❖ Dare to think beyond the boundaries you have yielded yourselves. Fantasy where does it come from?

❖ Osiris-Abydos Temple, aircraft, electrophoresis, unknown technology, DNA container, does this wake you up? Write it down, and share your knowledge with a world that craves.

❖ Sanskrit, Ashoka, the secret partnership of the nine men.

❖ In silence and veil, you will find your answers. Look into the depths of yourself.

❖ Dogon-people, DNA structures with twelve strings. Do you notice the changes in your body?

❖ Lemuria-light beings with no fixed form or structure. So it will be again.

❖ Energies on the inside of the pyramids in different countries from different dimensions - mirror images of the same. What do you see in your own mirror image?

❖ Recreation of an interdimensional network of energy and electromagnetism. Forecast track, be prepared.

❖ Navigation systems from antiquity to be recreated. Are you the one who will do the writings?

❖ Energy crystals, light balls, generator with information recorded with lasers light and sound in harmonious healing. Magnet structure that reverses the gravity. Memories of Atlantis. Does it make resonance and recall memories in you?

- ❖ The light carries information: Knowledge is so complete, that it is hard to put words to it.
- ❖ Light particles are human individual consciousness that is part of the great consciousness.
- ❖ Frequencies changed = frequency levels. Light has memory, light and thought frequency is the same
- ❖ Pyramids spirals-energy in the energy sphere spirals and pyramids, spiral in the head. Theta-gamma-spiral, Pyramid and David star multidimensional.
- ❖ Create life with light. Tidal waves of energy changes, leading to the physical DNA changes and changes in patterns of communication with other people, ref dolphins.
- ❖ Open up your inner ear. Opening the energy gates awakes DNA in the bodies, DNA are responding to the gates. Use the heart!
- ❖ Wormhole is travel routes in Star sectors.

❖ Makes each other stronger by using light, and stand in the power and infinity. Help each other in almighty; you just have to choose it!

❖ Leylines will be alive. Go to Egypt and search for 2012.

❖ Mind your unconscious action pattern, for this is the genuine unaffected pattern of humanity, as it is engraved in the wheels of time.

❖ Seven star systems

Anu from Star cluster Ceylon, South Pleiades

A good and a less good healer.

Once upon time there was a young lady named Amritha. This young lady was a light carrier and a natural born healer. At one time there was another lady named Liandy that wanted to heal this young lady. She needed practice and thought she would give Amritha a good experience. When the session started, Amritha god sick, she felt bad and lost her ability of using light in her own body. Liandy gave Amritha bad pictures in mind and physical changes. Amritha got so sick that she had to visit the medicine man in order to get healthy again. The medicine man told Amritha this: "The woman who did this could not use the energies that are coming from above. She was using her own energies and not the channeled energy that she was told to use. When this energy moved into her body, a block was created and she was not able to use it. She had to use her own personal energy to "heal". She is not a good healer, she needs to practice, she needs to learn more about herself and take a look at her own frequency. She carries around energies that are not good for sensitive people. The pictures were made to make Amritha understand, that this energy should not be used in a healing session. We must all learn from life and from our experiences. The book of Life is the book that truly matters. Some people are born with this wisdom, they do not need to learn, they just know. You sensitive, you are light creators and should not receive healing from people who are not light carriers like yourself, this is <u>very</u> important."

Amritha got healthy again but did for always remember the wisdom given to her. All light carriers have to walk their own miles in their own shoes. The Akashi records are the keepers of the contracts written before entering earth. Therefore we have different experiences to make.

Source: Geronimo, medicine man of the Appalachian people

Channeling
done by me.

The journey ahead, dear Light worker!

The journey will be like a boat on the open sea. Who knows what the sea will bring? It can go from stormy waters to be quiet in a flash. This is how it is going to be. Time will cease. The moment will be forever. What you decide will happen for your eyes, so be careful not to desire high waves, or just calm sea. Your decisions and thoughts will be all there is in the higher future.

The waves will be the mind and the sea will be the consciousness, on which you are going to sail on your journey. Select your ship and route with care, and join us for a wonderful new travel to the "end of the world" and beyond!

In the ocean of consciousness (to what is a sea here on earth) there will be creatures/aliens who will guide you on your way. They are known, and are part of the Sea of Consciousness and are an endless resource.

What lies behind and past is for us to know, and for you to find out. What we can tell with words and concepts that are understandable for you, is that you should walk with great care. Nothing is like you would expect, yet everything like you think and hope.

You will move through the space in between, and enjoy the momentarily joy and bliss it is, to be a part of everything. Have a rest, and be ready for a new adventure on new seas. Who knows where it will take you? **You** do. Believe. Have faith.

Source: The Boatman, The skipper, Noah.

"Where do you go from here?"

8. INFORMATION ABOT FUTURE BOOKS AND THE WORK AHEAD

The Owl man, the Book of Life

This is channeled information about our work.

Images are shown of the wisdom tree! This is "the book of life". In which dimension, in which time, when does this happen? Is it a symbol or is it tangible? It is a symbol! The hole in the tree holds many answers. The color blue is a clue. This book must be written in the nature. Natural forces will lead to the right crossroads.

The book should be written for people who need that special part that they are missing. This section is needed, to get ahead in their earthly life. You will know when this information appears and when to write it down. Other jobs to be done first! We slide, we pull in a different direction, to another destination!

You have to travel together. Travel together with us back in time. When particles were distributed and we were gone. Many of these particles got lost along the way, those few who survived ended up in people like you.

Some ended up in people which yet do not know. They have these particles in their earthly body today. Attention on the small things will be important! The small things will give you the big clues, wisdom and crossroads. Remember the word crossroad! This is not a physical road.

The symbols will be drawn! Symbols are not drawn yet – please note this! They shall be drawn — drawn by a child. A child who understand! Please pay attention to children's drawings in the future. The symbol is recognized when you see it. It will be recognized by a heat. There will be a heat radiation from this drawing.

Our destination for you on Earth has disappeared. That's what makes it difficult to create contact! The earthlings living in their own world. Many believe that this world is the only one. At this point, we say that it is wrong! There is life in other universes, in a different frequency, in other layers. We are part of this! The earthlings must learn to use their ancient powers correctly, they must learn to use light to the service of good. They must learn that darkness is not negative. There is a balance! Everything is balance!

The Earthlings must also learn how to start with themselves! It is impossible to help others on track, before the match is taken at your own level. We want to instruct, we want to help, and we will provide the light needed along the way! Humans and earthlings are two different things.

Energy fields that you radiate through mediation will evolve quickly! Please note! Error of interpretation may arise. Physical pain may seem threatening. Please note! This is not dangerous, there is a change. A change to the positive, to a new information source, into something higher – much higher than yourself! The power will flow, words will come.

The words are flowing through hands and through voice.

You have particles from many lives, many millennia, and many dimensions. Parts and imprints from different times and different places will be there. It will be felt and there will be a challenge to find out what's what. These particles will give fear. These Particles will give pleasure. It will be experienced in nightmares, and experienced in heavy situations that are to be turned around. They should be reversed to positive intent, to positive joy of life. Their mission will be to help other people to look at their own particles. See things in perspective! See the big picture and at the same time see details.

It's scratched in stone, but these are hidden, hence the "corridor". This knowledge has been the opposite of the public domain. This knowledge can be misused in the wrong hands. It can be used to put on a higher frequency, than what is sound for the earthly human. Some people contain particles from the Seidel clan in another sub frequency. This clan represents the opposite of the love frequency.

A new start — back to zero. The particles of this period are important to keep safe! Arrogance and abuse should not be used! Your mission is great! There will be people who want something different, which will stop you. It will be mockery, it will be laughing. At the same time, the most important thing that will be the outcome of this, is the satisfaction of accomplishing something directed by nature!

Take care of the children, those children who do not know who they are, why they are here. They are sent for! They are sent for to continue the work that is now being started. They should be taught to understand the importance of nature's own frequency!

Use this vibration to obtain new information from the new channels. The main channel and the most important now is the Destination Star 15. It is a lot lying dormant here! Take down with care. Note down what's happening around you at the same time as this information is captured. It will give clarity in the correlation! The needed context to understand and use this information.

"The book of Life" will be an aid. Request information from here and it will be given! Please note! It will be given through dreams, through images, experiences, and maybe also through channeled material. It has been a lot of information to you now, sort in 3 blocks: doctrinal parts, book material, its own rhythm and melody.

We have confidence, we believe and we have another type of love energy. This energy can only be felt by people with the right frequencies.

We look forward to working with you again.

"With love and wisdom, A helya - The" Owl man ".

"The Owl man"

Meditation – Journey to the fire in your heart!

(Non-physical plane of existence)

Let your heart tell you a story! Find a place where you can be alone. Sit or lie down and focus on your breathing.

Now it's time to travel to your heart frequency.

Let your heart tell you what really lives in you!

You are strong, you are loved and you are here for a reason!

Imagine the sky full of stars, stars that spread love over you and your life. One of the stars reaches out a hand and touches your skin. Feel the vibrancies!

Let it flow into your heart and open up! Let go of the sorrow, let go of the greed! Let your heart help you to reach your highest potential!

Make a picture of your "dream life". What is in it? Who is in it? What do you do? Where are you?

Remember that you are energy, you are love and passion! Make this be a part of what you truly believe!

Take a deep breath and put your hands over your heart. Imagine that you put all this love, passion and fire into your heart. Feel it with all your part in your body!

Now, when you are ready. Come back to your earth life and feel that your power has gone up to a new level!

YOU ARE LOVED!

Namaste

Ey ey kalel, ey ey aliash, aliash un ka ni!
(The language of light)

The writing process

Ever since 2008 the thought, both conscious and unconscious, as an always stronger urge to write, has crawled its way to our lives. Without knowing about each other and from different places, the tree of us has walked around doodling about this unexplainable need, to write books. The material that was about to be written was unknown, and odd to each and one of us.

In the beginning none of us dared to speak out loud about the book that was lurking in the back of our heads. When it turned out to be a full channeled book, we had hard times struggling with our disbeliefs and with our fears of being labeled as crazy. While working with the book, the fear passed and was replaced by inner love and light. There have been tears, there has been sorrow. The process of being free from oneself is worth battling.

In September 2009 a beautiful day arise over Oslo. At Bydgøyneset Marie Hofsløkken and Liv Christin Markussen met for the first time, ready to attend a course in[2] healing and health promoting work. We were completely unknown for each other and we had no clue about what life and the friendship to come had in store. Two years later, in august 2011, Silje Hostvedt Isaksen jumped into our lives. At Teveltunet, a beautiful mansion up in mountains of the North in Norway, Silje and Liv met during a spiritual course held by Lilli Bendriss, Camillo Løken and Anne-Marie Beck.

Under a week later the writing process escaladed. All of us have been standing with one leg in the spiritual world. Since childhood we have had different spiritual experiences. Nevertheless, the process of being channels for higher energies has been stretching, expanding and overwhelming for all

---

[2] Part time education over1,5 years in healing and health promoting work at The Paradigm Academy in Oslo, Norway.

of us. Proud and humble we now present the book to the audience.

"Learn to excel like you have been born to by finding the light within"

More information about us is to be found here:

www.thelightwithin.priv.no

Thank You for paying attention and for reading the book.

The Sources:

- ➤ The Great I Am / Pechama
- ➤ Sharak, Destination Star 15, Hercules family, galaxy 4783 in Corvus constellation, center of planet Nebula in The vermillion Bird of the south.
- ➤ Ashika, Destination Star 15
- ➤ Izrael, Destination Star 15
- ➤ Carmengadis Camaguru, alexia's galaxy nr, 3883, Leo constellation
- ➤ Gabriel, the Archangel
- ➤ Nefertiti
- ➤ The Dolphin spirit
- ➤ The sparkle of the Dolphins
- ➤ The higher Self
- ➤ White Eagle
- ➤ The Owl man
- ➤ Geronimo, The Medicine man
- ➤ Anu, Star cluster Ceylon, South-Pleiades
- ➤ Amin
- ➤ Noah

Made in the USA
Charleston, SC
17 November 2011